MASAOKA SHIKI

MODERN ASIAN LITERATURE

MASAOKA SHIKI

Selected Poems

TRANSLATED BY BURTON WATSON

COLUMBIA UNIVERSITY PRESS

NEW YORK

COLUMBIA UNIVERSITY PRESS
Publishers Since 1893
New York   Chichester, West Sussex
Copyright © 1997 Columbia University Press

Library of Congress Cataloging-in-Publica-
tion Data
Masaoka, Shiki, 1867–1902.
    [Poems. English. Selections]
    Masaoka Shiki : selected poems / trans-
lated by Burton Watson.
            p.   cm. — (Modern Asian litera-
ture)
    Includes bibliographical references.
    ISBN 978-0-231-11091-4 (ppr :   paper)

    1. Masaoka, Shiki, 1867–1902 — Trans-
lations into English.   2. Haiku —
Translations into English.   3. Waka —
Translations into English.   I. Watson,
Burton, 1925– .   II. Title.   III. Series.
PL811.A83A28   1997
895.6'142 — dc21   97-25799

CONTENTS

1867	Born in Matsuyama, Iyo Province (present-day Ehime Prefecture)
1868	Meiji Restoration
1870	Younger sister Ritsu born
1872	Father dies
1873	Enters elementary school, begins study of Chinese classics under maternal grandfather
1880	Enters Matsuyama Middle School
1883	Goes to Tokyo
1884	Enters University Preparatory School
1889	Coughs up blood, first sign of illness
1890	Enters literature department of Tokyo University
1891	Begins work on *Classified Collection of Haiku*
1892	Withdraws from university, becomes haiku editor of *Nippon*; beginning of haiku reform
1894	Outbreak of Sino-Japanese War (–1895)
1895	Goes to China as war correspondent for *Nippon*. Suffers severe lung hemorrhage on return trip in May. Hospitalized in Kobe, later moves to rest home in Suma. Goes to Matsuyama to convalesce, stays with Natsume Sōseki; returns to Tokyo in October
1898	Beginning of tanka reform; poetry meetings held at home
1899	Begins sketching plants and flowers; publishes *Haijin Buson*, influential study of haiku poet Yosa Buson
1900	Begins group study of *Manyō'shū*
1902	Illness becomes critical; dies at home on September 19

Although the Japanese had considerable acquaintance with the science and visual arts of the West before the Meiji Restoration in 1868, their knowledge of Western literature was extremely limited. With the official opening of the country in that year, however, and the flood of Western imports and influences that surged in from abroad, they soon found themselves confronted with a bewildering array of new literary forms and concepts.

As they gained increasing familiarity with Western literature, some Japanese writers began trying their hand at the new forms or endeavoring to apply these new approaches in their work. And in their initial enthusiasm for things foreign, some went so far as to opine that traditional Japanese literary forms such as *tanka* and *haiku* poetry, hopelessly enmeshed as they were in the culture of the past, were now obsolete and before long would pass out of existence.

Masaoka Shiki, who was born just one year before the Meiji Restoration, was among those who responded to these stimuli from the West with excitement and zeal. But, although he experimented with some of the new literary genres, he devoted most of his creative energy to reinvigorating the native haiku and tanka forms, endeavoring to free them from outworn conventions and make them viable media for artistic expression in the new era that was dawning in Japan. His labors played a significant role in bringing new vitality to the tanka form, and as a haiku poet, critic, and teacher he proved so successful that his compatriots now rank him among the four greatest writers to work in that medium.

Masaoka Shiki was born in Matsuyama on the island of Shikoku. His father, a samurai in the feudal domain of which Matsuyama was the castle town, died when Shiki was five, leaving his mother to bring up Shiki and his younger sister Ritsu. With the abolition of the feudal system that followed the Restoration, the family was left in a precarious financial situation and his mother had to take in sewing to help make ends meet. Shiki attended local schools in Matsuyama and also received instruction in the Chinese classics from his maternal grandfather, a Confucian scholar.

From childhood Shiki had a passion for literature, but his Confucian training led him to view it as insufficiently dignified for a lifetime career. Being an enthusiastic supporter of the new peoples' rights movement, he considered going into politics but later determined to study law or philosophy.

To do so, he felt it imperative that he somehow get to Tokyo, where all the important social and intellectual ferment of the nation was centered, though poverty seemed to render that impossible. In 1883, however, an uncle living in Tokyo arranged for him to come to the capital, where he won a scholarship for boys of samurai descent from the former Matsuyama domain and entered University Preparatory School. Though he was a rather mediocre scholar whose literary enthusiasms constantly lured him away from other studies, in time he was able to enroll in the literature department of Tokyo University. He withdrew in 1892, his second year, to devote full time to creative activities.

He had started writing poems in haiku form around 1884, and his interest in the medium continued to grow, though he received no formal training in it. In 1891 he set about educating himself in the history of the form by reading all the collections of earlier haiku he could lay hands on, a course of study that provided the foundation for his critical writings on haiku and led in time to the completion of a work entitled *Haiku bunrui* (Classified Collection of Haiku). Late in 1892, after withdrawing from Tokyo University, he became haiku editor for the newspaper *Nippon*, to which he had contributed earlier, an association that was to last his lifetime.

When the Sino-Japanese War broke out in 1894 Shiki, eager to join the action, volunteered for a job as war correspondent for his newspaper. As early as 1889 he had coughed up blood from his lungs, the first sign of the tuberculosis that would eventually prove fatal. Subsequently, he had shown further symptoms of the disease, but he refused to let considerations of health deter him. By the time he arrived in China in the spring of 1895, however, hostilities had ended. He spent a month sightseeing in the Dairen and Chin-chou area, a fact reflected in some of the poems in the selection that follows. During the return voyage to Japan he suffered a severe hemorrhage of the lungs and on arrival in Kobe was rushed to a hospital. Family and friends gathered around what they expected would be his deathbed, but he rallied miraculously and soon left the hospital for a rest home in nearby Suma, a spot that appears frequently in his poems. By late summer he was back in Matsuyama, though his mother and sister had by this time moved to Tokyo.

In Matsuyama he stayed with his friend Natsume Sōseki, who was later to become the most distinguished novelist of the Meiji period, and led a group of friends and admirers in the study and writing of haiku. In October he returned to Tokyo and resumed work with *Nippon*, publishing his own haiku and those of like-minded poets, along with critical works, in its pages during the years that followed.

By this time the tuberculosis had settled in his spine and was not only causing him immense discomfort but making walking all but impossible. Confined to bed most of the time, he devoted all his energies to literary pursuits—writing poems, critical pieces, and diaries—and joined with friends and followers who gathered in his sickroom to discuss literature. His mother and sister kept house and looked after him as best they could, an increasingly difficult task as his condition worsened.

In 1898 he began efforts to reform the tanka, publishing critical remarks on tanka, writing tanka, and proceeding much as he had in his earlier campaign to reinvigorate the haiku. But often he was in such severe pain that he could barely concentrate on his work. His only real relief came from the doses of morphine he took several times a day. Toward the end of his life he spent time each day, when the morphine had momentarily quelled the pain, sketching a flower, fruit, or vegetable that had been placed at his bedside, one of the last expressions of his inexhaustible engagement with and passion for the world around him. In 1902 his condition rapidly deteriorated and he died in September of that year, a few weeks short of his thirty-fifth birthday.

It is ironic that the haiku, which many people in Shiki's day thought would wither away under the impact of new literary forms from abroad, has now become one of Japan's most successful cultural exports. In recent years the form has been taken up with enthusiasm in America and other countries of the West, so that there is now scarcely any need to explain to readers of English what a haiku is.

The haiku was originally part of a longer form, the *renga*, or "linked verse," a type of poem composed jointly by two or more persons who took turns contributing "links," or sections, of the poem. Known by the term *hokku*, or "starting verse," the haiku constituted the first section of the longer poem and was hence of special importance. It was made up of three units of five, seven, and five syllables or sound symbols, respectively, and always included a *kigo*, or "season word," indicating the season of the year the lines depicted. This last was important because it allowed readers to visualize the sights, sounds, and weather conditions associated with that particular season and hence with the images embodied in the lines. Because of the extreme brevity of the form, writers of hokku, or haiku, have had to rely heavily upon such associations to bring across to readers the scene and mood they wish to convey.

In his efforts to rejuvenate the haiku form Shiki did not question the use of the 5–7–5 sound pattern or of the season word, though later reformers were to jettison both these formal requirements.[1] What he did first of all was to establish the haiku as completely separate from the renga, a poetic form fully capable of standing on its own. To emphasize this step, he rejected the older term *hokku*, as well as *haikai*, another term by which the form was known in earlier times, and replaced them with the designation *haiku*.

In response to criticisms that the seventeen-syllable form was simply too brief for serious artistic expression, particularly in comparison with the longer forms being introduced from the West, Shiki argued that its very brevity was its strength and that as a result it was capable of types of expression impossible in other forms.

Although the hokku, technically speaking, was simply the opening section of a renga, there had been a tendency from early times to treat some hokku as independent poems or to compose hokku that had no renga continuation. The first poet to compose hokku of true depth and artistic stature was Matsuo Bashō (1644–1694), who is regarded by many as the greatest haiku poet of all time. His famous poem on the frog jumping into an old pond is a prime example of a hokku that has always been treated as an independent poem. Two other poets in the years following who wrote haiku of outstanding quality were Yosa Buson (1716–1783) and Kobayashi Issa (1763–1827). These three, along with Masaoka Shiki, make up the four masters of the form mentioned earlier. But few poets of the age could measure up to the standard exemplified by these men, and there were literally thousands of haiku poets of the Edo period (1600–1867), when the form enjoyed its greatest

[1] Like many other haiku writers, Shiki did at times depart slightly from the 5–7–5 pattern for artistic purposes.

vogue, who produced little more than lifeless imitations of Bashō's works or compositions devoid of serious artistic intent. Because of its brevity and formal simplicity, the haiku was frequently treated merely as a vehicle for wordplay, amusing satire, or downright vulgarity, particularly among the members of the townsman class.

The haiku had thus sunk to a very low level of inspiration and literary worth when Shiki came on the scene. Shiki had from the first been interested in all types of literature, uncertain as to what genre he wished to focus on. In his student days he wrote a short novel, but when he showed it to one of the leading fiction writers of the day, the response was not encouraging. Since he had for some time written haiku, he decided to see what he could do to inject new vitality and seriousness into that form.

He was greatly aided in these efforts by the fact that he had never for any appreciable time studied under a professional teacher of haiku and thus was not allied with any of the traditional schools or teaching lines of haiku writing. He was able to approach the form as an outsider, viewing it objectively and freely offering whatever suggestions for improvement seemed pertinent. And with his suggestions went examples from his own hand of how he thought they should be applied.

Most of the advice Shiki offered to haiku writers was quite simple, even commonplace, and could have been applied to almost any literary genre. He urged them first of all not to be bound by the conventions of the past but to be open and natural in their approach and to endeavor to create works that conformed first of all to their own tastes. They were to broaden the scope of their work, not limiting themselves to time-worn themes but incorporating material from their daily lives, no matter how humdrum.

Borrowing from the vocabulary of Western painting, he adopted the term *shasei*, or "sketch from life," to describe the technique that underlies much of his own poetry and prose. The writer was to carry out minute observation of the scenes around him and to compose works based on what he saw there, conjuring up the mood or emotional tenor he desired through apt manipulation of the images found in real life. As Shiki advised poets in a piece called *Zuimon zuitō* (Random Questions and Random Answers) written in 1899: "Take your materials from what is around you—if you see a dandelion, write about it; if it's misty, write about the mist. The materials for poetry are all about you in profusion."[2]

In his younger days, when he still enjoyed good health, Shiki took a number of walking trips through different parts of Japan, carrying out just such a process of observation and recording his impressions in poems and prose journals. In his later, bedridden years his observations were limited almost entirely to his sickroom and the small garden that adjoined it, yet he continued until the very end to draw artistic inspiration from the few flowers, plants, and other objects that were within his field of vision. Or he wrote about the foods he enjoyed, particularly such fruits as persimmons, since eating was one of the few physical pleasures that his ailment had not deprived him of.

Shiki in his haiku for the most part rejected puns, wordplays, allusions to earlier literature, or poems that "tell a little story"—techniques much relied on by many previous haiku writers—in favor of straightforward realism. Within the limits he set himself, however, he tried for a wide variety of effects.

On occasion he concentrated entirely on the natural scene, as in this poem:

Fluttering, fluttering,
butterflies yellow
over the water

[2] Quotation translated in Janine Beichman, *Masaoka Shiki* (reprint; Tokyo: Kodansha International, 1986), p. 46.

At other times his haiku are more akin to *senryū*, the humorous or satirical poems in haiku form that focus on human activities:

> Sounds of snoring—
> a plate and a sake bottle
> set outside the mosquito net

The curious interrelatedness or seeming interrelatedness of phenomena is often a key element in his work, as in the famous poem:

> I eat a persimmon
> and a bell starts booming—
> Hōryū-ji

Buddhism is a religion profoundly concerned with causes and conditions, and the poem is set at one of the oldest and most venerable of the country's Buddhist temples, Hōryū-ji in Nara. Is Shiki telling us that there is some arcane connection between the eating of the persimmon and the sounding of the bell?

Some of Shiki's poems appear to comment on the state of the times:

> Ripening in fields
> that once were the samurai quarter—
> autumn eggplant

Others are as starkly noncommittal as a Cubist painting:

> A red apple
> a green apple
> on top of the table

Though many of Shiki's poems clearly are based on scenes that were before him at the time of writing, others draw upon memories of the past or are partly or wholly imaginary. But whatever the genesis of the poem, whatever its components, we sense in it always Shiki's unflagging search for meaningfulness, his longing to create an artistic moment the significance of which will far transcend the elements that go into it.

As mentioned earlier, Shiki used his column in *Nippon* to publish his own haiku and those of fellow poets, as well as critical writings. The caustic and controversial nature of some of his pronouncements soon attracted attention, and in time his work and that of his followers, which came to be known as the Nippon school of haiku, from the name of the newspaper, gained recognition as a significant part of the literary scene.

Shiki started writing poetry in tanka form as early as 1882, and in 1898 he began serious efforts to reinvigorate it. The tanka, or "short poem," also known by the more general term *waka*, or "Japanese poem," consists of thirty-one syllables arranged in a pattern of 5–7–5–7–7 syllables. It is far older than the haiku form, dating back to the earliest period of recorded literature, and has traditionally been associated in particular with the court aristocracy. Unlike the haiku, which often employed colloquial expressions, the tanka limited itself to the refined diction of classical Japanese and was even more convention bound and wedded to the themes and sentiments of the past than the haiku.

Shiki's effort to reform the tanka followed the same general approach he had employed with the haiku: an appeal for greater freedom and naturalness in the handling of the form, for greater realism in subject matter. Once again, to illustrate his recommendations he accompanied them with examples of his own compositions in the form.

In the end, Shiki's tanka reforms proved to be less significant than his earlier efforts with the haiku, in part because he was not the only one endeavoring to open up new avenues of expression for the tanka, and because his illness robbed him of the time and energy needed to press forward with his reforms. Nevertheless, he exerted an important influence on the development of the tanka and left some deeply moving works in the form, such as the famous ten-poem sequence on the wisteria flowers in the selection that follows.

To call Shiki a prolific poet seems an almost laughable understatement. He is said to have written some two thousand poems in tanka form and more than twenty-five thousand haiku, more than four thousand of the latter in one year, 1893. One must keep in mind, however, that we are speaking about forms of great brevity. The very large number of poems in his oeuvre reflects the restless fertility of his artistic imagination, his belief that a poet must be constantly experimenting and probing for new themes and modes of expression, and the care he took to preserve his works and those of the other poets with whom he was associated. He believed that bad poems as well as good should be recorded so that one could learn from one's mistakes.

How does a translator make a selection from such a staggering number of poems? Clearly, if he is not to spend a lifetime at the task he must rely on choices made by Japanese editors, in order to ascertain which poems the Japanese themselves have regarded as outstanding and to avoid having to read through all the poems in Shiki's corpus that are of only limited interest and appeal. Because of their strongly occasional nature, Shiki's poems are sometimes so closely tied to the particular circumstances of composition that they have little meaning for the general reader.

In my own selection I have tried to include a number of his more famous works, though some of these seemed to require too much background explanation to be effective in translation, or for some other reason resisted the transition into concise and intelligible English. At the same time I have not hesitated to include works that strike me as appealing, though they may not be so highly esteemed by connoisseurs in the field.

The haiku is much too short to express ideas and was never intended for that purpose. Its aim, as Shiki himself stresses, is to convey to the reader a certain mood or emotion, and when it does that effectively, I for one experience a sort of tingling sensation. Sometimes this seems to be because the poem calls up so vividly a scene or situation I have known in Japan or reminds me of something from my childhood; at times it is because the poem presents some unusual or arresting juxtaposition of images; and in other cases I am hard pressed to say just what makes the work so moving. It is principally poems of this inexplicably evocative, highly electric type that I have tried to include, though many of them may on the surface appear rather plain or even banal in expression. Janine Beichman in the volume cited earlier remarks that, "Shiki worked with the small, the finite, the close to home."[3] Precisely for that reason, however, he seems to come across, to me at least, with greater impact than those poets whose works move on a more grandiose plane.

Because Shiki greatly broadened the subject matter of the haiku and tanka forms by introducing themes and images never treated before—the drabber details of daily life or new importations such as baseball or glass doors—some critics have complained that his works are shallow or lacking in poetic overtones. But those who open up new artistic territory are almost always vulnerable to such charges; patina comes only with age. We should be grateful to Shiki for the risks he took in breaking new ground.

My selection is made up of 144 haiku, 34 tanka, and 4 *kanshi*, or poems in classical Chinese. Thanks to the excellent training in Chinese that Shiki received from his grandfather, he was able to write traditional-style Chinese verse with considerable ease, and during his boyhood days in Matsuyama he often composed kanshi with his school friends. In later years he employed the form much less frequently, and thus most of his kanshi fall into the category of juvenilia. The poems in Chinese I have translated date from his more mature years, though they retain traces of his youthful romanticism.

[3] Ibid., p. 72.

The poems in my selection are arranged in chronological order within the three divisions of haiku, tanka, and kanshi. Nearly all Shiki's poems can be dated with accuracy, and such an arrangement will allow readers to observe his stylistic growth and see how the illness of his later years curtailed the range of subject matter and otherwise affected his poetry. Shiki is careful to include a season word in all his haiku; therefore, for the benefit of readers who may not be thoroughly familiar with the indicators of seasonal change in Japan, I have noted the season to which the poem belongs. In Shiki's later haiku the season words play a particularly poignant role: as he came to realize that his sickness was incurable, they function as a kind of ominous clock relentlessly ticking away the time left to him.

In making my selection and writing this introduction, I have profited greatly from the study by Janine Beichman cited earlier. It contains excellent discussions of Shiki's life and literary work, as well as many translations from his poetry, critical writings, diaries, and other prose pieces. Anyone interested in Shiki should consult it by all means. Other works that have been helpful to me or that are recommended to readers are listed in the bibliography at the end of the book.

Many years ago, when I was a graduate student in Kyoto University and people would ask me what my research topic was, I would reply, "Shiki." If the inquirers knew that I was enrolled in the Department of Chinese Language and Literature, they would usually understand my reply to mean that I was making a study of the *Shih chi* (pronounced *Shiki* in Japanese), the *Records of the Historian*, a voluminous history of ancient China written by Ssu-ma Ch'ien (145?–89? B.C.E.). But sometimes in response to my answer the other party would begin making seemingly irrelevant remarks about haiku or Meiji period literature, and it would dawn on me that the inquirer had mistaken my "Shiki" to mean the poet Masaoka Shiki.

In due course I produced a book on Ssu-ma Ch'ien's *Shih chi* and went on to translate parts of his history. But it never occurred to me that one day I might also do a book on the other Shiki, Masaoka. Some years later, however, when Hiroaki Sato and I were compiling an anthology of Japanese poetry in translation, he asked me to translate a selection of Masaoka Shiki's poems for the book. In the process of doing so, I developed a great fondness for Shiki's work and decided that at some future date I would do a whole book on it. The present volume is the result.

Those earlier translations, which appeared in our anthology *From the Country of Eight Islands* (Doubleday & Company, 1981; Columbia University Press, 1988), are included here with minor revisions, along with a large number of new translations. One of the kanshi translations appeared in my *Japanese Literature in Chinese*, vol. 2 (Columbia University Press, 1976).

Some decades before Ezra Pound, with his injunction to "Make it new!", set about infusing new spirit into poetry in the English language, Masaoka Shiki, young as he was, was urging his compatriots to take similar steps to rescue the traditional Japanese poetic forms from their moribund state. Shiki, sad to say, was not blessed with Pound's longevity, and perhaps never fully realized his artistic potential, but he left behind a body of poetry that is remarkable for its acute observation and aptness of expression. In his younger days he was brash and outspoken, but with a sense of humor and intense dedication to his undertakings that somehow compensated for his imperiousness; toward the end he was difficult, as those who are in constant pain and discomfort often are. But it is clear that, given the circumstances fate dealt him, he did his best to produce lasting works of literature and to help those around him to do likewise. I hope that the translations presented here will enable readers of English to gain a deeper appreciation of this remarkable man and his work.

HAIKU

1891 SUMMER

1.

Hydrangeas —
and rain beating down
on the crumbled wall

1891 SUMMER

2.

In cleft on cleft,
on rock face after rock face —
wild azaleas

1. *ajisai ya / kabe no kuzure o / shibuku ame*
2. *iwa iwa no / wareme wareme ya / yama-tsutsuji*

1892 SUMMER

3.

Slipping out
the back way,
cooling off by the river

1892 SUMMER

4.

From the firefly
in my hands,
cold light

3.   *nukeura o / nukete kawabe no / suzumi kana*
4.   *te no uchi ni / hotaru tsumetaki / hikari kana*

1892 AUTUMN

5.

Singing somewhere
back of the shoe closet—
a katydid

1892 AUTUMN

6.

Autumn leaves flanking it
on either side,
a raft headed downstream

5.   *getabako no / oku ni nakikeri / kirigirisu*
6.   *ryōgan no / momiji ni kudasu / ikada kana*

1892 WINTER

7.

Winter winds—
the creaky noise the kettle makes
hanging from its hook

1892 WINTER

8.

Rustling softly
over the bamboo—
snow in the night

7.   *kogarashi ya / jizai ni kama no / kishiru oto*
8.   *sara-sara to / take ni oto ari / yoru no yuki*

1893 NEW YEAR'S

9.

Deep in the mountains—
New Year's decorations on the gate
of a house where no one calls

1893 WINTER

10.

Lonely sound—
simmering in the firepit,
wood chips with snow on them

9.   *okuyama ya / hito konu ie no / kado-kazari*
10.   *wabishisa ya / irori ni nieru / hota no yuki*

1893 WINTER

11.

From a rear window
in the falling snow
a woman's face looks out

1893 SPRING

12.

Deserted temple
where the bell's been stolen—
cherries just opening

11.   *uramado no / yuki ni kao dasu / onna kana*
12.   *mujūji no / kane nusumarete / hatsuzakura*

1893 SPRING

13.

Under my sandal soles
the sweet smell
of meadow grasses

1893 SPRING

14.

In the light of an evening moon
shelves of silkworms
faintly white

13.   *nobe no kusa / zōri no ura ni / kōbashiki*
14.   *yūzuki ya / hono-bono shiroki / kaiko-dana*

1893 SUMMER

15.

The wind blows,
the duckweed moves,
blooming all the while

1893 SUMMER

16.

Cool summer darkness—
laughing voices
on the far side of the river

15.   *kaze fuite / ukikusa ugoku / hana nagara*
16.   *yami-suzushi / kawa no mukō no / waraigoe*

1893 SUMMER

17.

Tenement house —
mosquito repellent smoldering
in every window down the row

1893 SUMMER

18.

Sounds of snoring —
a plate and a sake bottle
set outside the mosquito net

17.   *mado narabu / nagaya tsuzuki no / kayari kana*
18.   *ibiki ari / sara mo tokuri mo / kaya no soto*

1893 SUMMER

19. At an Inn

> Sudden downpour—
> and all these maids
> hauling out storm shutters

1893 SUMMER

20.

> Such stillness—
> a spring, its waters
> whirling up grains of sand

19.   *yūdachi ya / amado kuridasu / gejo no kazu*
20.   *shizukasa wa / suna fukiaguru / izumi kana*

1893 SUMMER

21.

Above the treetops
far away
fireworks explode

1893 SUMMER

22.

Lotuses
blooming there—
the lonely train station

21.   *ki no sue ni / tōku no hanabi / hirakikeri*
22.   *hasu no hana / saku ya sabishiki teishajō*

1893 SUMMER

23.

Water striders—
all but washed away,
they dart back upstream

1893 SUMMER

24.

Pressing my bare body
up against the plaster wall—
this heat!

23.   *mizusumashi / nagaren to shite / tobikaeru*
24.   *hadakami no / kabe ni hittsuku / atsusa kana*

1893 AUTUMN

25.

Long night,
when the waterfall
makes all kinds of noises

1893 AUTUMN

26.

Scarecrow—
his back to you
any way you look at him

25.   *taki no ne no / iro-iro ni naru / yonaga kana*
26.   *dochira kara / mitemo ushiro no / kakashi kana*

1893 AUTUMN

27.

A carp leaps up,
crinkling
the autumn moonlight

1894 SUMMER

28.

Always someone resting there—
a lone rock
in the summer field

27.　*koi hanete / tsuki no sazanami / tsukurikeri*
28.　*taezu hito / ikou natsuno no / ishi hitotsu*

1894 AUTUMN

29.

Stone Buddha standing there—
fallen leaves settled
in his hands

1894 WINTER

30. Looking at a Picture of Bashō

I here by the stove,
you off on
your wanderings

29. *ote no ue ni / ochiba tamarinu / tachibotoke*
30. *ware wa kotatsu / kimi wa angya no / sugata kana*

1894 WINTER

31.

Five-story pagoda
looming up through
the leafless trees of winter

1895 SPRING

32.

A train goes by,
its smoke curling
around the new tree leaves

31.   *fuyu kodachi / gojū no tō no / sobiekeri*
32.   *kisha sugite / kemuri uzumaku / wakaba kana*

1895 SPRING

33.

A whole bucket of indigo dye
dumped into it—
the spring river

1895 SPRING

34.

Picture of the Buddha
entering nirvana—
one person is laughing!*

---

*Pictures of the Buddha "entering nirvana" (i.e., on his deathbed) typically show him lying on his side surrounded by monks, gods, animals, birds, and other beings—all weeping and lamenting inconsolably.

33. *hito-oke no / ai nagashikeri / haru no kawa*
34. *nehanzō / hotoke hitori wa / waraikeri*

1895 SPRING

35.

One penny
and you get to ring the temple
    bell—
noonday haze

1895 SPRING

36. Chin-chou*

Pears in bloom—
a wrecked house
left from the battle

*A city near Dairen in the Liaotung Peninsula in China where Shiki went as war correspondent in April 1895, immediately after the end of the Sino-Japanese War.

35.   *issen no / tsurigane tataku ya / hirugasumi*
36.   *nashi saku ya / ikusa no ato no / kuzure-ie*

1895 SPRING

37.

Fluttering, fluttering,
butterflies yellow
over the water

1895 SPRING

38.

Dead squid
with the ink it spit out—
low tide

37. *hira-hira to / chōchō ki nari / mizu no ue*
38. *sumi haite / ika no shiniiru / shiohi kana*

1895 SPRING

39.

Where the castle stood,
daikon radish
blooming on top of the hill

1895 SUMMER

40. In Suma

At daybreak
a white sail goes by
outside my mosquito net

39. *shiro ato ya / daikon hana saku / yama no ue*
40. *akebono ya / shiraho sugiyuku / kaya no soto*

1895 SUMMER

41. In Suma

> My summer jacket
> wants to get rid of me
> and fly away

1895 SUMMER

42. Suma Temple

> I toss in two coins,
> borrow the temple porch
> to cool off on

41. *natsu-baori / ware o hanarete / toban to su*
42. *nimon nagete / tera no en karu / suzumi kana*

1895 SUMMER

43.

So cool—
even through the hole in the stone
    lantern,
the sea

1895 SUMMER

44. Suma Temple

Buddha too—
he's opened his altar doors,
cooling off

43.   *suzushisa ya / ishidōrō no / ana mo umi*
44.   *mihotoke mo / tobira o akete / suzumi kana*

1895 SUMMER

45.

Hedges blooming
with rose of sharon—
in the alley, a ladder seller

1895 SUMMER

46.

Poppies open,
and the same day
shatter in the wind

45.   *mukuge saku / kaki ya komichi no / hashigo-uri*
46.   *keshi saite / sono hi no kaze ni / chirinikeri*

1895 SUMMER

47.

People going home—
after the fireworks
it's so dark!

1895 SUMMER

48.

To ears
muddied with sermons,
a cuckoo*

---

*By "sermons" here Shiki probably means sermonizing, particularly on the subject of artistic theory and practice. The cuckoo teaches a more natural and unstudied way.

47.   *hito kaeru / hanabi no ato no / kurasa kana*
48.   *sekkyō ni / kegareta mimi o / hototogisu*

1895 AUTUMN

49.

Sunset sky—
people crowding around
the sardine nets

1895 AUTUMN

50.

After I squashed
the spider—
lonely night chill

49. *yūyake ya / iwashi no ami ni / hitodakari*
50. *kumo korosu / ato no sabishiki / yosamu kana*

1895 AUTUMN

51. Stopping at a Teashop at Hōryū-ji Temple

> I eat a persimmon
> and a bell starts booming—
> Hōryū-ji

1895 AUTUMN

52.

> Autumn passes—
> for me no gods
> no buddhas

51. *kaki kueba / kane ga narunari / Hōryū-ji*
52. *yuku aki no / ware ni kami nashi / hotoke nashi*

1895 AUTUMN

52.

Ripening in fields
that once were the samurai
    quarter—
autumn eggplant

1895 AUTUMN

53.

Round paper fan discarded—
the face of the geisha
looks so sad

52. *buke machi no / hatake ni narinu / aki nasubi*
53. *sute-uchiwa / yūjo no kao no / aware nari*

1895 AUTUMN

54. Taking Leave of Sōseki*

> For me, who go,
> for you who stay behind—
> two autumns

1895 WINTER

55. Nara

> Buddhas—
> a thousand years' grime on them
> and no one wipes it off

---

*The novelist Natsume Sōseki (1867–1916), who at this time was a middle school teacher in Matsuyama. Shiki was leaving Matsuyama for Tokyo.

54.   *yuku ware ni / todomaru nare ni / aki futatsu*
55.   *sennen no / susu mo harawazu / hotoketachi*

1895 WINTER

56.

Sawing hunks of charcoal,
my little sister's hands
are all black!

1895 WINTER

57.

Winter rice fields—
railroad tracks running
a level above them

56.   *nokogiri ni / sumi kiru imo no / te zo kuroki*
57.   *kishadō no / ichidan takaki / fuyuta kana*

1895 WINTER

58.

Getting lazy—
taking my socks off
after I get in bed

1895 WINTER

59.

Hands so cold
I can't work the writing brush—
nearing midnight

58. *bushōsa ya / futon no naka de / tabi o nugu*
59. *te kogoete / fude ugokazu yo ya / fukenuran*

1895 WINTER

60.

Morning sun lighting them—
long ones, short ones,
icicles under the eaves

1895 WINTER

61.

Year-end housecleaning—
gods and buddhas
sitting out on the grass

60.   *hi no sasu ya / noki no tsurara no / naga-mijika*
61.   *susuhaki ya / kami mo hotoke mo / kusa no ue*

1896 SPRING

62.

Spilling its pink
in the spring breeze—
tooth powder

1896 SPRING

63.

Below the bedding
hung out to air—
strawberry blossoms white

62.   *harukaze ni / koborete akashi / hamigaki-ko*
63.   *futon hosu / shita ni ichigo no / hana shiroshi*

1896 SPRING

64.

Little country store—
warm with the steam
from red beans and rice

1896 SPRING

65.

Forsythia—
branches tied up out of the way
in a corner of the garden

64. *sekihan no / yuge atataka ni / no no komise*
65. *rengyō ya / tabaneraretaru / niwa no sumi*

1896 SUMMER

66.

Country road—
boys whacking at a snake,
barley-harvest time

1896 SUMMER

67.

Amid a jumble of
tanka books, haiku books—
noonday nap

66.   *no no michi ya / warabe hebi utsu / mugi no aki*
67.   *kasho haisho / funzen to shite / hirune kana*

1896 SUMMER

68.

Summer storm—
all the sheets of blank paper
blown off my desk

1896 SUMMER

69.

Swatting mosquitoes—
blood stains
on the war tale I'm reading

68. *natsu arashi / kijō no hakushi / tobitsukusu*
69. *ka o utte / gunsho no ue ni / chi o in su*

1896 SUMMER

70.

Sky blazing—
as I go down the gravel path,
husks of dead butterflies

1896 AUTUMN

71.

Chilly nights—
at the public bath
someone went off with my clogs

70.   *enten ya / jarimichi yukeba / chō no kara*
71.   *sentō de / geta kaeraruru / yosamu kana*

1896 AUTUMN

72.

Temple gate
creak-creaking as they close it—
autumn evening

1896 AUTUMN

73.

Lightning flash—
in the bottom of the basin,
water someone forgot to throw out

72.   *sammon o / gii to tozasu ya / aki no kure*
73.   *inazuma ya / tarai no soko no / wasure-mizu*

1896 AUTUMN

74.

Garden ten paces long—
no corner
where fall winds don't blow

1896 AUTUMN

75.

Blowy autumn evening—
can't keep my mind
on the book I'm reading

74.   *niwa jippo / aki kaze fukanu / kuma mo nashi*
75.   *nowaki no yo / fumi yomu kokoro / sadamarazu*

1896 AUTUMN

76.

Morning fog—
one man's got a fire going—
construction workers' shed

1896 AUTUMN

77.

A little window—
autumn sun going down
beyond the honey locust trees

76.   *asagiri ya / hitori hi o taku / fushin-goya*
77.   *saikachi ni / aki no hi otsuru / komado kana*

1896 AUTUMN

78.

The little knife—
sharpening pencils with it,
peeling pears

1896 AUTUMN

79.

Peeling pears—
sweet juice drips
from the knife blade

78.   *kogatana ya / empitsu o kezuri / nashi o muku*
79.   *nashi muku ya / amaki shizuku no / ha o taruru*

1896 WINTER

80.

Old garden—
in the moonlight, dumping out
water from a hot-water bottle

1896 WINTER

81. Sickbed Snowfall: Four Poems (1)*

It's snowing!
I can see it through the hole
in the shoji

*For Shiki, coming from Matsuyama in Shikoku, a snowfall was a rare and exciting phenomenon.

80.   *furuniwa ya . . ıki ni tampo no / yu o kobosu*
81.   *yuki furu yo / shōji no ana o / mite areba*

1896 WINTER

82. Sickbed Snowfall: Four Poems (2)

I keep asking
how deep
the snow's gotten

1896 WINTER

83. Sickbed Snowfall: Four Poems (3)

All I can think of
is lying here
in a house with all this snow

82. *ikutabi mo / yuki no fukasa o / tazunekeri*
83. *yuki no ie ni / nete iru to omou / bakari nite*

1896 WINTER

84. Sickbed Snowfall: Four Poems (4)

Open the shoji—
let me get a good look
at this Ueno snow!

1896 WINTER

85.

Stalks of dried pampas grass—
when I open the shoji
they beckon to me

84.   *shōji akeyo / Ueno no yuki o / hitome min*
85.   *karesusuki / shōji akureba / ware o maneku*

1897 SUMMER

86.

Airing books—
today I'll do
the haiku collections

1897 SUMMER

87.

Thunderstorm over,
a lone tree in the evening sun,
the cry of a cicada

86. *mushi-boshi ya / kyō wa haisho no / kashū no bu*
87. *rai harete / ichiju no yūhi / semi no koe*

1897 SUMMER

88. Sick in Bed

Crows at four,
sparrows at five—
and then the summer night is over

1897 AUTUMN

89.

Twilight cicadas—
the shadow of the pasania tree
presses on my desk

*An example of a poem that departs significantly from the 5–7–5 sound pattern.

88. *yoji ni karasu / goji ni suzume / natsu no yo wa akenu**
89. *higurashi ya / tsukue o assu / shii no kage*

1897 AUTUMN

90.

Persimmons made me think of it—
the face of the maid
at that inn in Nara

1897 AUTUMN

91. Working All Day and into the Night to Clear Out My Haiku Box

I checked
three thousand haiku
on two persimmons

90.   *kaki ni omou / Nara no hatago no / gejo no kao*
91.   *sanzen no / haiku o kemishi / kaki futatsu*

1897 AUTUMN

92.

Coming to pick up
pasania nuts—
kids from next door

1897 AUTUMN

93. After I'm Dead

Tell them
I was a persimmon eater
who liked haiku

92. *shii no mi o / hiroi ni kuru ya / tonari no ko*
93. *kaki kui no / haiku konomishi to / tsutau beshi*

1897 AUTUMN

94.

I pulled on a creeper
and all this fruit
came falling down

1897 AUTUMN

95.

This year
I took sick with the peonies,
got up with the chrysanthemums

94. *tsuru kusa o / hikeba shitataka ni / mi no otsuru*
95. *ware kotoshi / botan ni yande / kiku ni okishi*

1897 WINTER

96.

In the bud vase
from France,
a winter rose

1897 WINTER

97. Sent to Hekigotō, who is in the hospital with smallpox*

Cold, I bet—
itchy, I bet—
and wishing for company too

---

* Kawahigashi Hekigotō (1873–1937) was one of Shiki's closest friends and followers.

96. *Furansu no / ichirinzashi ya / fuyu no bara*
97. *samukarō / kayukarō hito ni / aitakarō*

1898 NEW YEAR'S

98.

It too has a New Year's wreath—
the back door
where the tradespeople come

1898 WINTER

99.

Talking to myself,
hugging a hot water bottle
gone tepid

98.   *wakazari ya / chōnin hairu / katteguchi*
99.   *hitorigoto / nuruki tampo o / kakaekeri*

1898 SPRING

100.

Forsythia blossoms scattered,
leaves of the plantain
still unfurled

1898 SPRING

101.

Little child,
soles of her feet green
from the grass she walked in

100.   *rengyō wa / chitte tama maku / bashō kana*
101.   *osanago ya / aoki o fumishi / ashi no ura*

1898 SUMMER

102.

Drying on
bindweed blossoms,
a passing shower

1898 SUMMER

103. Feeling a Little Better

Put the chair there—
where my knees
will touch the roses

102.   *hirugao no / hana ni kawaku / tōriame*
103.   *isu o oku ya / sōbi ni hiza no / fururu toko*

1898 SUMMER

104.

The little red-light district
in the harbor where the boats tie
    up —
cotton in bloom

1898 SUMMER

105.

trumpet vine —
upstairs back room
in a hotspring inn

104.   *funatsuki no / chisaki kuruwa ya / wata no hana*
105.   *nōzen ya / ideyu no yado no / ura nikai*

1898 SUMMER

106.

As the rickshaw enters
the wooded stretch,
a shower of locust cries

1898 SUMMER

107.

Recovering, yes—
but eyes so tired
just looking at roses!

106.   *jinriki no / mori ni hairu ya / semi-shigure*
107.   *bara o miru / me no kutabire ya / yamiagari*

1898 SUMMER

108.

Summer grass—
in the distance
people playing baseball

1898 AUTUMN

109.

Autumn moon shining in—
reaching even beyond
the people playing go

108.   *natsugusa ya / bēsu-bōru no / hito tōshi*
109.   *tsuki sasu ya / go o utsu hito no / ushiro made*

1898 WINTER

110.

Gusts of winter wind—
pine needles strewn
all over the outdoor Noh stage

1899 SPRING

111.

A single peak,
snow still on it—
there where the province ends

110.   *kogarashi ya / matsuba fukichiru / nōbutai*
111.   *yuki nokoru / itadaki hitotsu / kuni-zakai*

1899 SUMMER

112.

I think I'll die
eating apples,
in the presence of peonies

1899 SUMMER

113.

In the creek,
reed blinds shielding it—
a melon we're chilling

112. *ringo kūte / botan no mae ni / shinan kana*
113. *yoshizu shite / kakou nagare ya / hiyashi-uri*

1899 AUTUMN

114.

Persimmons strung up to dry,
in front of the shed
back of the bath

1899 AUTUMN

115.

Fall rains—
scum collecting on
the garden pool

114. *hoshigaki ya / yudono no ushiro / naya no mae*
115. *aki ame ya / misabi no tamaru / niwa no ike*

1899 AUTUMN

116. I Bought My First Cane

> With the help of a cane
> I actually stood up—
> bushclover blossoms

1899 AUTUMN

117.

> Cockscombs—
> all of them knocked flat
> in the autumn storm

116.   *tsue ni yorite / tachi-agarikeri / hagi no hana*
117.   *keitō no / mina taoretaru / nowaki kana*

1899 WINTER

118.

A stray cat
is shitting
in my winter garden

1899 WINTER

119.

Winter moon—
above the bare trees
the morning star

118. *nora-neko no / fun shite iru ya / fuyu no niwa*
119. *kangetsu ya / kareki no ue no / hitotsu-boshi*

1899 WINTER

120.

Fingertips yellow
from peeling tangerines—
a winter shut-in

1899 WINTER

121.

Through the glass door
the winter sun shines in—
sickroom

120. *mikan hagu / tsuma-saki ki nari / fuyugomori*
121. *garasu-goshi ni / fuyu no hi ataru / byōma kana*

1900 NEW YEAR'S

122.

New Year's well-wishers—
five or six
around a sickbed

1900 NEW YEAR'S

123.

Back from the first play
of the season,
not yet out of her holiday clothes

122. *byōshō o / kakomu reisha ya / gorokunin*
123. *hatsu-shibai / mite kite haregi / imada nugazu*

1900 NEW YEAR'S

124.

Blank sheets stitched together—
my poetry notebook
for the year ahead

1900 SPRING

125.

Washing green onions—
where the meadow creek
comes into town

124.   *shinnen no / shiro-kami tojitaru / kuchō kana*
125.   *negi arau ya / nogawa no machi ni / iru tokoro*

1900 SUMMER

126.

A red apple
a green apple
on top of the table

1900 AUTUMN

127.

Crickets—
in the corner of the garden
where we buried the dog

126.   *akaki ringo / aoki ringo ya / taku no ue*
127.   *kōrogi ya / inu o uzumeshi / niwa no sumi*

1900 WINTER

128.

Winter solstice—
how beautiful the cakes
on the Buddhist altar!

1900 WINTER

129.

Writing brush so stubby,
the words are all blurred
in my winter diary

128.   *butsudan no / kashi utsukushiki / tōji kana*
129.   *fude chibite / kasureshi fuyu no / nikki kana*

1901 AUTUMN

130.

Plunging into
a ripe persimmon—
getting my beard all messy with it

1901 AUTUMN

131.

For eating persimmons too,
I think this year
may be my last

130. *kaburitsuku / jukushi ya hige o / yogoshikeri*
131. *kaki kuu mo / kotoshi bakari to / omoikeri*

1901 AUTUMN

132.

The sumo wrestler,
old now,
who never made it to *ōzeki**

1901 WINTER

133.

Clog with a broken thong
discarded in the
winter paddy

* The second highest rank in sumo wrestling.

132.   *ōzeki ni / nara de oinuru / sumō kana*
133.   *o no kireshi / geta sutete aru / fuyuta kana*

1902 NEW YEAR'S

134. In My Room (Dictated from a Sickbed)

> The Blue Cliff Record
> incomprehensible as ever
> on a bellyful of *zōni**

1902 WINTER

135. In My Room (Dictated from a Sickbed)

> Coldest time of the year—
> but the tangerine I eat
> after I take my medicine!

---

*The Blue Cliff Record, *Hekiganshū* or *Hekiganroku*, is a Chinese collection of Zen koans noted for its paradoxical language. *Zōni* is a soup of vegetables and rice cake eaten on New Year's morning.

134.   *kai shikanuru / Hekiganshū ya / zōni-bara*
135.   *kusuri nomu / ato no mikan ya / kan no uchi*

1902 WINTER

136.

Wild ducks settled into sleep
on Shinobazu Pond—
frosty evening

1902 SPRING

137.

Home alone,
my mother off cherry-viewing—
I watch the clock

136. *Shinobazu no / kamo neshizumaru / shimo-yo kana*
137. *tarachine no / hanami no rusu ya / tokei miru*

1902 SUMMER

138.

The sound of scissors
clipping roses—
a clear spell in May

1902 SUMMER

139.

They've cut down the willow—
the kingfishers
don't come anymore

138.   *bara o kiru / hasami no oto ya / satsukibare*
139.   *yanagi kitte / kawasemi tsui ni / kozu narinu*

1902 SUMMER

140.

Sketching from life—
eggplants are harder to do
than pumpkins

1902 AUTUMN

141.

Daily routine,
sketching a plant or flower—
we're into autumn

140.   *kabocha yori / nasu muzukashiki / shasei kana*
141.   *kusabana o / egaku nikka ya / aki ni iru*

1902 AUTUMN

142.

Rice cooked with chestnuts—
and the yellow of the
sponge gourd blossoms

1902 AUTUMN

143.

Now and then
lifting my head to look—
bushclover in the garden

142.   *kurimeshi ya / hechima no hana no / ki naru ari*
143.   *kubi agete / ori-ori miru ya / niwa no hagi*

1902 AUTUMN

144.

A purple so deep
it's almost black—
the grapes

144. *kuroki made ni / murasaki fukaki / budō kana*

TANKA

1897

145. Reverend Guan Sent Me Fifteen Persimmons from
His Garden*

> Some of the persimmons
> are sweet tasting,
> some of the persimmons
> are puckery—
> the puckery ones are best!

1898

146. Scene outside Chin-chou City

> No one to bury
> the bodies
> of the dead soldiers—
> mountain road in spring,
> violets blooming

---

* Amata Guan (1854–1904), a Zen monk living in Kyoto.

145. *kaki no mi no / amaki mo arinu / kaki no mi no / shibuki mo arinu / shi-buki zo umaki*
146. *mononofu no / shikabane osamuru / hito mo nashi / sumire hana saku / haru no yamamichi*

1898

147. Chin-chou, After the War

There are houses
in the mountain shade
but no one lives there—
lone village,
its willows turned green

1898

148.

In the old garden
bush clover and pampas grass
put out new shoots—
it's time for
my sickness to mend!

147. *yamakage ni / ie wa aredomo / hito sumanu / koson no yanagi / midori shinikeri*

148. *furuniwa no / hagi mo susuki mo / me o fukinu / yamai iyubeki / toki wa kinikeri*

1898

149.

Orange tree by the window
where I lie sick—
its blossoms open and scatter,
its fruits appear,
and still I lie here sick

1898

150.

Potted plants, two—
the deep purple I think
is columbine,
the red flower
I've forgotten the name of

149.   *yamite fusu / mado no tachibana / hana sakite / chirite mi ni narite /*
       nao yamite fusu
150.   *hachi futatsu / murasaki koki wa / odamaki ka / akaki wa hana no / na*
       o wasurekeri

1898

151.

Fall winds that raged
the whole night through
died away at dawn—
my little sister straightens up
the fence with the morning glories

1898

152.

Village sunk in sleep,
lights all gone out,
the Milky Way
white
over groves of bamboo

151.   *yoru hito-yo / areshi nowaki no / asa-nagite / imo ga hikiokosu / asagao no kaki*
152.   *neshizumaru / sato no tomoshibi / mina kiete / ama-no-gawa shiroshi / takeyabu no ue ni*

1898

153. A Dream in Sickness

I was so happy—
I'd climbed Mount Fuji,
feet trembling
on its summit—
and then the dream ended

1898

154. I Who

I who
hear the drums
from Yoshiwara*
and alone late at night
sort out haiku

* A famous brothel district near Shiki's house in Tokyo

153. *ureshikumo / noborishi Fuji no / itadaki ni / ashi wananakite / yume sa-men to su*

154. *Yoshiwara no / taiko kikoete / fukuru yo ni / hitori haiku o / bunrui su ware wa*

1898

155. I Who

I who
listen to a man
tell how he climbed
Mount Fuji
and rub my skinny legs

1898

156. I Who

I who
think so often of
the fun I had as a boy,
and watch the fireworks
more intently than a child

155.   *Fuji o fumite / kaerishi hito no / monogatari / kikitsutsu hosoki / ashi sa-suru ware wa*
156.   *mukashi seshi / warabe-asobi o / natsukashimi / ko yori hanabi ni / yo-nen nashi ware wa*

1898

157. I Who

I who,
when others are all off
having fun in
Hakone or Ikaho,
sit home swatting flies

1898

158. I Who

. I who
plant the pit
in the little garden,
waiting for the time when a tree
will flower and bear fruit

---

157. *hito mina no / Hakone Ikaho to / asobu hi o / io ni komorite / hae kor-*
      osu ware wa
158. *kudamono no / tane o koniwa ni / makiokite / hana saki minoru / toshi o*
      matsu ware wa

1899

159. Sick in Bed, Delighted by Fair Weather

Still in bed,
I get them to open the rain shut-
    ters,
reveling in the clear spell,
groves of Ueno with
morning sun bright on them

1900

160. Groves of Trees

When evening settles
over Ueno Hill,
groves of trees darken,
and in the garden of wild beasts
the wild beasts roar*

Kedamono no sono or "garden of wild beasts" is Shiki's somewhat fanciful term for the Ueno Zoo, established in 1882.

159.   *fushinagara / amado akesase / asahi teru / Ueno no mori no / hare o yorokobu*

160.   *Ueno yama / yū koekureba / mori kurami / kedamono hoyuru / kedamono no sono*

1900

161. The Glass Window*

Glass door
in my sickroom
I can peer right through—
I see sparrows darting among
the branches of the little pines

1900

162. The Glass Window

Through the glass window
in my sickroom
winter sun streams in—
my good luck plant†
is blooming

---

*Takahama Kyoshi (1874–1959), one of Shiki's principal disciples, arranged to have glass installed in the sliding doors of Shiki's room in December of 1899. Shiki refers to it variously as a door or a window. Glass was still at this time a rarity. First of a set of twelve poems with this title.

†*Fukujusō*, or "good fortune long life plant," a small ornamental plant with yellow blossoms, associated with the New Year's season.

161.   *itatsuki no / neya no garasudo / kage sukite / komatsu no eda ni / suzume tobu miyu*

162.   *itatsuki no / neya no garasu no / mado no uchi ni / fuyu no hi sashite / sachikusa sakinu*

1900

163. The Glass Window

Wiping moisture
from the glass door
by the sickbed where I spend the
   winter
I see tabi socks
hanging out to dry

1900

164. The Glass Window

That crow on the platform
where we hang the wash—
is he cawing because
he sees me through the glass door,
writing in my room?

163. *fuyugomoru / yamai no toko no / garasudo no / kumori nugueba / tabi hoseru miyu*
164. *monohoshi ni / kiiru karasu wa / garasudo no / uchi ni fumi kaku / ware mite naku ka*

1900

165.

Red shoots of roses
reaching out two feet—
their thorns are soft
in the falling
spring rain

1900

166.

Beyond the hedge
where I heard
a train go by,
smoke swirls up over
the tops of the budding trees

165.   *kurenai no / nishaku nobitaru / bara no me no / hari yawaraka ni / haru-*
        same no furu
166.   *kisha no ne no / hashirisugitaru / kaki no soto no / moyuru konure ni /*
        kemuri uzumaku

1900

167. Written on Seeing the Garden Pines in the Rain on the
Morning of May 21st*

> Pine needles,
> each needle strung with its
> drop of bright dew,
> forming, then falling,
> falling, then forming again

1900

168. Stars

> Stars numberless
> as grains of sand—
> one among them
> shining
> straight at me

---

* Second in a series of ten poems with this title.

167.   *matsu no ha no / ha goto ni musubu / shiratsuyu no / okite wa kobore /
       koborete wa oku*
168.   *masago nasu / kazu naki hoshi no / sono naka ni / ware ni mukaite / hi-
       karu hoshi ari*

1901

169. Ten-Poem Sequence on the Wisteria Blossoms* (1)

I had finished eating supper and was lying face up in bed when I noticed the vase of wisteria on the desk to my left. The flowers had drawn up plenty of water and were now at their finest. What elegance, what loveliness! I exclaimed to myself, and before I knew it I was recalling the romantic tales of long ago. And then, oddly enough, I felt inspired to write some poems in tanka form. These days I've pretty much neglected this practice, so it was with some uncertainty that I took up my brush.

> The sprays of wisteria
> arranged in the vase
> are so short
> they don't reach
> to the tatami†

---

* The prose introduction and poems are from Shiki's diary *Bokujū itteki* (A Drop of Ink), 1901.

† The straw matting on the floor of the room.

169.   *kame ni sasu / fuji no hanabusa / mijikakereba / tatami no ue ni / todo-kazarikeri*

1901

170. Ten-Poem Sequence on the Wisteria Blossoms (2)

> The sprays of wisteria
> arranged in a vase—
> one cluster
> dangles down
> on the piled-up books

1901

171. Ten-Poem Sequence on the Wisteria Blossoms (3)

> When I look
> at the wisteria blossoms
> I think with longing of far-off
>   times,
> the Nara emperors,
> the emperors of Kyoto

170.   *kame ni sasu / fuji no hanabusa / hitofusa wa / kasaneshi fumi no / ue ni taretari*

171.   *fuji nami no / hana o shi mireba / Nara no mikado / Kyō no mikado no / inishie koishi mo*

1901

172. Ten-Poem Sequence on the Wisteria Blossoms (4)

When I look
at wisteria blossoms
I want to get out
my purple paints
and paint them

1901

173. Ten-Poem Sequence on the Wisteria Blossoms (5)

If I were to paint
the purple
of the wisteria blossoms,
I ought to paint it
a deep purple

172. *fuji nami no / hana o shi mireba / murasaki no / enogu toriide / utsusan to omou*

173. *fuji nami no / hana no murasaki / e ni kakaba / koki murasaki ni / kaku-bekarikeri*

1901

174. Ten-Poem Sequence on the Wisteria Blossoms (6)

Sprays of wisteria
arranged in a vase—
the blossoms hang down,
and by my sickbed
spring is coming to an end

1901

175. Ten-Poem Sequence on the Wisteria Blossoms (7)

Last year in spring
I saw the wisterias
in Kameido—
seeing this wisteria now,
I recall it

174. *kame ni sasu / fuji no hanabusa / hana tarete / yamai no toko ni / haru kuren to su*
175. *kozo no haru / Kamedo ni fuji o / mishi koto o / ima fuji o mite / omoii-detsumo*

1901

176. Ten-Poem Sequence on the Wisteria Blossoms (8)

> Before the
> red blossoms
> of the peonies,
> the wisteria's purple
> comes into bloom

1901

177. Ten-Poem Sequence on the Wisteria Blossoms (9)

> These wisterias
> have blossomed early—
> the Kameido wisterias
> won't be out for
> ten days or more

176. *kurenai no / botan no hana ni / sakidachite / fuji no murasaki / sakiide-nikeri*

177. *kono fuji wa / hayaku sakitari / Kameido no / fuji sakamaku wa / tōka mari nochi*

1901

178. Ten-Poem Sequence on the Wisteria Blossoms (10)

> If you stick the stems
> in strong sake
> the wilted flowers
> of the wisteria
> will bloom again like new

1902

179.

> I don't know when
> I'll get well again,
> but I'm having seeds
> for fall flowers
> planted in the garden

178. *yashiōri no / sake ni hitaseba / shioretaru / fuji nami no hana / yomi-gaeri saku*
179. *itatsuki no / iyuru hi shira ni / saniwabe ni / aki kusabana no / tane o makashimu*

KANSHI

(7-CH. REGULATED
VERSE; 1890)

180. Sojourn at Mii Temple*

How many times have dreams brought me winging to this site?
Ten days' borrowed lodging, brushwood gate closed.
Green peaks, tier on tier, come down from north and east,
endless expanse of white cloud bordering the capital region.
Sudden shower beyond the railing, a pair of swallows dart by;
in a corner of the lake broken rainbows, a solitary sail returning.
The mountain monk at twilight has tolled the bell and gone off—
echoes linger over the water, fainter and fainter to the ear.

* Temple near Kyoto situated on a hill overlooking Lake Biwa.

(7-CH. *CHÜEH-CHÜ*; 1895)

181. Chin-chou City

Flags and pennants, a hundred thousand, swept the sky;
one battle, a nation undone, bare bones heaped up.
Dogs bark in empty compounds, people a desolate few.
Wind and rain fill the city where apricot blossoms unfold.

(5-CH. OLD STYLE; 1895)

182. Up after Illness

Liaotung, following the horses of war;
taken sick on the ship back home,
two months laid up in Kobe,
dried bones, a youthful mind in ashes.
Where did my wandering eyes turn to?
I headed for the post station of Suma,
free and easy, idling under clear skies,
up mornings, again toward evening.
Morning and evening I lean on the railing,
breezes springing up from the edge of the sky.
Green pines hold a glimpse of sea color,
a white sail tags after the sound of rain.
Before I know it the sound of rain passes,
dirt and grim washed all away.
A scrap of cloud sinks below the blue waves;
radiant, the moon like a mirror.
The mirror moon lights my eyebrows,
my mind communes with the gods,
long shouts circling ten thousand miles,
sword-keen ambitions crammed in my chest.

(5-CH. OLD STYLE; 1896)

183. Poor Man's Hut

Poor man's hut—still room for my knees,
shelf stacked with a hundred volumes;
on the west wall an old painting hanging,
arhat with eyeballs lightning bright;
east wall, lines from the *Li sao*,*
a rainbow descending in blazoned hues;
straw raincoat, hat with old words written on it;
precious sword, memento of old battles—
high hopes of youth bit by bit ground down,
I envy myself the wanderings I once had.
Cramped and cringing, I never go out the gate,
thinking only how the rounding years go by.
Bamboo breath—congelation of green cloud;
plum blossoms—a spatter of white snow;
sunlight dimly rays the north window;
ice spreads its stiff crust over my iron inkstand.
Heedless of Heaven, headless of men,
all I do is peck and polish away at my writings,
but words differ from east to west
and tastes of today belie those of the past.
My sentences are as ineffectual as the otter's sacrifice,†
my poems as pointless as a winter fan.
My one room opens to the north;

* "Encountering Sorrow," a long rhapsodic poem by the Chinese poet Ch'ü Yüan of the third century B.C.E.

† According to ancient Chinese belief, the otter is performing a "sacrifice" when it leaves part of its prey uneaten.

wind from the door crack pricks my face.
My mother lives here too—
fifty years old and never worn silk—
bustling bustling beside the blue lamp,
stitching clothes, eyes fixed on thread and needle.
I have no two acres of land—
couldn't retire to a life of farming.
I have no talent for saving the world—
could never put on official's cap.
"Poor means stupid!" people say—
down and out, I wince at their nasty saw.

Beichman, Janine. *Masaoka Shiki*. Boston: Twayne, 1982; Tokyo: Kodansha International, 1986.

Blyth, Reginald Horace. *A History of Haiku*. Tokyo: Hokuseido Press, 1964.

Bowers, Faubion, trans. *The Classic Tradition of Haiku: An Anthology*. Mineola, NY: Dover Publications, Inc., 1996.

Bownas, Geoffrey, and Anthony Thwaite, trans. *The Penguin Book of Japanese Verse*. Baltimore: Penguin Books, 1964.

Brower, Robert H. *Tradition and Modernization in Japanese Culture*. Princeton: Princeton University Press, 1971.

Carter, Steven D., trans. *Traditional Japanese Poetry*. Stanford: Stanford University Press, 1991.

Cohen, William Howard. *To Walk in Seasons: An Introduction to Haiku*. Rutland, VT: C. E. Tuttle Co., 1972.

Hamill, Sam. *The Sound of Water: Haiku by Basho, Buson, Issa, and Other Poets*. Boston: Shambala, 1995.

Henderson, Harold. *An Introduction to Haiku*. Garden City, NY: Doubleday & Co., 1958.

Higginson, William J. *The Haiku Handbook*. Tokyo: Kodansha International, 1989.

Isaacson, Harold J. *Peonies Kana: Haiku by the Upasaka Shiki*. New York: Theatre Arts Books, 1972.

Keene, Donald, trans. *Dawn to the West: Japanese Literature in the Modern Era*. New York: Holt, Rinehart & Winston, 1984.

———. "Shiki and Takuboku." In his *Landscapes and Portraits*. Tokyo: Kodansha International, 1971.

———. "Masaoka Shiki." In his *Some Japanese Portraits*. Tokyo: Kodansha International, 1978.

———. "The Diaries of Masaoka Shiki." In his *Modern Japanese Diaries*. New York: Henry Holt, 1995.

Miner, Earl. *Japanese Poetic Diaries*. Berkeley: University of California Press, 1969.

Miyamori, Asataro, trans. *Masterpieces of Japanese Poetry, Ancient and Modern*. Tokyo: Maruzen, 1932; Westport, CT: Greenwood Press, 1970.

Morris, Mark, "Buson and Shiki," *Harvard Journal of Asiatic Studies*, vol. 44, no. 2 (1984) and vol. 45, no. 1 (1985).

Sato, Hiroaki, and Burton Watson, eds. *From the Country of Eight Islands*. Garden City, NY: Anchor Press, 1981; Seattle: University of Washington Press, 1981; New York: Columbia University Press, 1986.

Ueda, Makoto. "Masaoka Shiki." In his *Modern Japanese Poets and the Nature of Literature*. Stanford: Stanford University Press, 1983.

———. *Modern Japanese Haiku: An Anthology*. Toronto: University of Toronto Press, 1976.

———. *Modern Japanese Tanka: An Anthology*. New York: Columbia University Press, 1996.

Viglielmo, V. H. *Japanese Literature in the Meiji Era*. Tokyo: Obunsha, 1955.

TRANSLATIONS FROM THE ASIAN CLASSICS

Major Plays of Chikamatsu, tr. Donald Keene 1961

Four Major Plays of Chikamatsu, tr. Donald Keene. Paperback ed. only. 1961

Records of the Grand Historian of China, translated from the Shih chi of Ssu-ma Ch'ien, tr. Burton Watson, 2 vols. 1961

Instructions for Practical Living and Other Neo-Confucian Writings by Wang Yang-ming, tr. Wing-tsit Chan 1963

Hsün Tzu: Basic Writings, tr. Burton Watson, paperback ed. only. 1963

Chuang Tzu: Basic Writings, tr. Burton Watson, paperback ed. only. 1964

The Mahābhārata, tr. Chakravarthi V. Narasimhan. Also in paperback ed. 1965

The Manyōshū, Nippon Gakujutsu Shinkōkai ed. 1965

Su Tung-p'o: Selections from a Sung Dynasty Poet, tr. Burton Watson. Also in paperback ed. 1965

Bhartrihari: Poems, tr. Barbara Stoler Miller. Also in paperback ed. 1967

Basic Writings of Mo Tzu, Hsün Tzu, and Han Fei Tzu, tr. Burton Watson. Also in separate paperback eds. 1967

The Awakening of Faith, Attributed to Aśvaghosha, tr. Yoshito S. Hakeda. Also in paperback ed. 1967

Reflections on Things at Hand: The Neo-Confucian Anthology, comp. Chu Hsi and Lü Tsu-ch'ien, tr. Wing-tsit Chan 1967

The Platform Sutra of the Sixth Patriarch, tr. Philip B. Yampolsky. Also in paperback ed. 1967

Essays in Idleness: The Tsurezuregusa of Kenkō, tr. Donald Keene. Also in paperback ed. 1967

The Pillow Book of Sei Shōnagon, tr. Ivan Morris, 2 vols. 1967

Two Plays of Ancient India: The Little Clay Cart and the Minister's Seal, tr. J. A. B. van Buitenen 1968

The Complete Works of Chuang Tzu, tr. Burton Watson 1968

The Romance of the Western Chamber (Hsi Hsiang chi), tr. S. I. Hsiung. Also in paperback ed. 1968

The Manyōshū, Nippon Gakujutsu Shinkōkai edition. Paperback ed. only. 1969

Records of the Historian: Chapters from the Shih chi of Ssu-ma Ch'ien, tr. Burton Watson. Paperback ed. only. 1969

Cold Mountain: 100 Poems by the T'ang Poet Han-shan, tr. Burton Watson. Also in paperback ed. 1970

Twenty Plays of the Nō Theatre, ed. Donald Keene. Also in paperback ed. 1970

Chūshingura: The Treasury of Loyal Retainers, tr. Donald Keene. Also in paperback ed. 1971

The Zen Master Hakuin: Selected Writings, tr. Philip B. Yampolsky 1971

Chinese Rhyme-Prose: Poems in the Fu Form from the Han and Six Dynasties Periods, tr. Burton Watson. Also in paperback ed. 1971

Kūkai: Major Works, tr. Yoshito S. Hakeda. Also in paperback ed. 1972

The Old Man Who Does as He Pleases: Selections from the Poetry and Prose of Lu Yu, tr. Burton Watson 1973

The Lion's Roar of Queen Śrīmālā,tr. Alex and Hideko Wayman 1974

Courtier and Commoner in Ancient China: Selections from the History of the Former Han by Pan Ku, tr. Burton Watson. Also in paperback ed. 1974

Japanese Literature in Chinese, vol. 1: Poetry and Prose in Chinese by Japanese Writers of the Early Period, tr. Burton Watson 1975

Japanese Literature in Chinese, vol. 2: Poetry and Prose in Chinese by Japanese Writers of the Later Period, tr. Burton Watson 1976

Scripture of the Lotus Blossom of the Fine Dharma, tr. Leon Hurvitz. Also in paperback ed. 1976

Love Song of the Dark Lord: Jayadeva's Gītagovinda, tr. Barbara Stoler Miller. Also in paperback ed. Cloth ed. includes critical text of the Sanskrit. 1977

Ryōkan: Zen Monk-Poet of Japan, tr. Burton Watson 1977

Calming the Mind and Discerning the Real: From the Lam rim chen mo of Tson-kha-pa, tr. Alex Wayman 1978

The Hermit and the Love-Thief: Sanskrit Poems of Bhartrihari and Bilhaṇa, tr. Barbara Stoler Miller 1978

The Lute: Kao Ming's P'i-p'a chi, tr. Jean Mulligan. Also in paperback ed. 1980

A Chronicle of Gods and Sovereigns: Jinnō Shōtōki of Kitabatake Chikafusa, tr. H. Paul Varley. 1980

Among the Flowers: The Hua-chien chi, tr. Lois Fusek 1982

Grass Hill: Poems and Prose by the Japanese Monk Gensei, tr. Burton Watson 1983

Doctors, Diviners, and Magicians of Ancient China: Biographies of Fang-shih, tr. Kenneth J. DeWoskin. Also in paperback ed. 1983

Theater of Memory: The Plays of Kālidāsa, ed. Barbara Stoler Miller. Also in paperback ed. 1984

The Columbia Book of Chinese Poetry: From Early Times to the Thirteenth Century, ed. and tr. Burton Watson. Also in paperback ed. 1984

Poems of Love and War: From the Eight Anthologies and the Ten Long Poems of Classical Tamil, tr. A. K. Ramanujan. Also in paperback ed. 1985

The Bhagavad Gita: Krishna's Counsel in Time of War, tr. Barbara Stoler Miller 1986

The Columbia Book of Later Chinese Poetry, ed. and tr. Jonathan Chaves. Also in paperback ed. 1986

The Tso Chuan: Selections from China's Oldest Narrative History, tr. Burton Watson 1989

Waiting for the Wind: Thirty-six Poets of Japan's Late Medieval Age, tr. Steven Carter 1989

Selected Writings of Nichiren, ed. Philip B. Yampolsky 1990

Saigyō, Poems of a Mountain Home, tr. Burton Watson 1990

The Book of Lieh-Tzŭ: A Classic of the Tao, tr. A. C. Graham. Morningside ed. 1990

The Tale of an Anklet: An Epic of South India—The Cilappatikāram of Iḷaṅkō Aṭikaḷ, tr. R. Parthasarathy 1993

Waiting for the Dawn: A Plan for the Prince, tr. and introduction by Wm. Theodore de Bary 1993

Yoshitsune and the Thousand Cherry Trees: A Masterpiece of the Eighteenth-Century Japanese Puppet Theater, tr., annotated, and with introduction by Stanleigh H. Jones, Jr. 1993

The Lotus Sutra, tr. Burton Watson. Also in paperback ed. 1993

The Classic of Changes: A New Translation of the I Ching as Interpreted by Wang Bi, tr. Richard John Lynn 1994

Beyond Spring: T'zu Poems of the Sung Dynasty, tr. Julie Landau 1994

The Columbia Anthology of Traditional Chinese Literature, ed. Victor H. Mair 1994

Scenes for Mandarins: The Elite Theater of the Ming, tr. Cyril Birch 1995

Letters of Nichiren, ed. Philip B. Yampolsky; tr. Burton Watson et al. 1996

Unforgotten Dreams: Poems by the Zen Monk Shōtetsu, tr. Steven D. Carter 1997

The Vimalakirti Sutra, tr. by Burton Watson 1997

MODERN ASIAN LITERATURE SERIES

Modern Japanese Drama: An Anthology, ed. and tr. Ted. Takaya. Also in paperback ed. 1979

Mask and Sword: Two Plays for the Contemporary Japanese Theater, by Yamazaki Masakazu, tr. J. Thomas Rimer 1980

Yokomitsu Riichi, Modernist, Dennis Keene 1980

Nepali Visions, Nepali Dreams: The Poetry of Laxmiprasad Devkota, tr. David Rubin 1980

Literature of the Hundred Flowers, vol. 1: *Criticism and Polemics*, ed. Hualing Nieh 1981

Literature of the Hundred Flowers, vol. 2: *Poetry and Fiction*, ed. Hualing Nieh 1981

Modern Chinese Stories and Novellas, 1919 1949, ed. Joseph S. M. Lau, C. T. Hsia, and Leo Ou-fan Lee. Also in paperback ed. 1984

A View by the Sea, by Yasuoka Shōtarō, tr. Kären Wigen Lewis 1984

Other Worlds; Arishima Takeo and the Bounds of Modern Japanese Fiction, by Paul Anderer 1984

Selected Poems of Sŏ Chŏngju, tr. with introduction by David R. McCann 1989

The Sting of Life: Four Contemporary Japanese Novelists, by Van C. Gessel 1989

Stories of Osaka Life, by Oda Sakunosuke, tr. Burton Watson 1990

The Bodhisattva, or Samantabhadra, by Ishikawa Jun, tr. with introduction by William Jefferson Tyler 1990

The Travels of Lao Ts'an, by Liu T'ieh-yün, tr. Harold Shadick. Morningside ed. 1990

Three Plays by Kōbō Abe, tr. with introduction by Donald Keene 1993

The Columbia Anthology of Modern Chinese Literature, ed. Joseph S. M. Lau and Howard Goldblatt 1995

Modern Japanese Tanka, ed. and tr. by Makoto Ueda 1996

STUDIES IN ASIAN CULTURE

The Ōnin War: History of Its Origins and Background, with a Selective Translation of the Chronicle of Ōnin, by H. Paul Varley 1967

Chinese Government in Ming Times: Seven Studies, ed. Charles O. Hucker 1969

The Actors' Analects (Yakusha Rongo), ed. and tr. by Charles J. Dunn and Bungō Torigoe 1969

Self and Society in Ming Thought, by Wm. Theodore de Bary and the Conference on Ming Thought. Also in paperback ed. 1970

A History of Islamic Philosophy, by Majid Fakhry, 2d ed. 1983

Phantasies of a Love Thief: The Caurapañcāśikā Attributed to Bilhaṇa, by Barbara Stoler Miller 1971

Iqbal: Poet-Philosopher of Pakistan, ed. Hafeez Malik 1971

The Golden Tradition: An Anthology of Urdu Poetry, ed. and tr. Ahmed Ali. Also in paperback ed. 1973

Conquerors and Confucians: Aspects of Political Change in Late Yüan China, by John W. Dardess 1973

The Unfolding of Neo-Confucianism, by Wm. Theodore de Bary and the Conference on Seventeenth-Century Chinese Thought. Also in paperback ed. 1975

To Acquire Wisdom: The Way of Wang Yang-ming, by Julia Ching 1976

Gods, Priests, and Warriors: The Bhṛgus of the Mahābhārata, by Robert P. Goldman 1977

Mei Yao-ch'en and the Development of Early Sung Poetry, by Jonathan Chaves 1976

The Legend of Semimaru, Blind Musician of Japan, by Susan Matisoff 1977

Sir Sayyid Ahmad Khan and Muslim Modernization in India and Pakistan, by Hafeez Malik 1980

The Khilafat Movement: Religious Symbolism and Political Mobilization in India, by Gail Minault 1982

The World of K'ung Shang-jen: A Man of Letters in Early Ch'ing China, by Richard Strassberg 1983

The Lotus Boat: The Origins of Chinese Tz'u Poetry in T'ang Popular Culture, by Marsha L. Wagner 1984

Expressions of Self in Chinese Literature, ed. Robert E. Hegel and Richard C. Hessney 1985

Songs for the Bride: Women's Voices and Wedding Rites of Rural India, by W. G. Archer; eds. Barbara Stoler Miller and Mildred Archer 1986

A Heritage of Kings: One Man's Monarchy in the Confucian World, by JaHyun Kim Haboush 1988

COMPANIONS TO ASIAN STUDIES

Approaches to the Oriental Classics, ed. Wm. Theodore de Bary 1959

Early Chinese Literature, by Burton Watson. Also in paperback ed. 1962

Approaches to Asian Civilizations, eds. Wm. Theodore de Bary and Ainslie T. Embree 1964

The Classic Chinese Novel: A Critical Introduction, by C. T. Hsia. Also in paperback ed. 1968

Chinese Lyricism: Shih Poetry from the Second to the Twelfth Century, tr. Burton Watson. Also in paperback ed. 1971

A Syllabus of Indian Civilization, by Leonard A. Gordon and Barbara Stoler Miller 1971

Twentieth-Century Chinese Stories, ed. C. T. Hsia and Joseph S. M. Lau. Also in paperback ed. 1971

A Syllabus of Chinese Civilization, by J. Mason Gentzler, 2d ed. 1972

A Syllabus of Japanese Civilization, by H. Paul Varley, 2d ed. 1972

An Introduction to Chinese Civilization, ed. John Meskill, with the assistance of J. Mason Gentzler 1973

An Introduction to Japanese Civilization, ed. Arthur E. Tiedemann 1974

Ukifune: Love in the Tale of Genji, ed. Andrew Pekarik 1982

The Pleasures of Japanese Literature, by Donald Keene 1988

A Guide to Oriental Classics, eds. Wm. Theodore de Bary and Ainslie T. Embree; 3d edition ed. Amy Vladeck Heinrich, 2 vols. 1989

INTRODUCTION TO ASIAN CIVILIZATIONS

Wm. Theodore de Bary, General Editor

Sources of Japanese Tradition, 1958; paperback ed., 2 vols., 1964

Sources of Indian Tradition, 1958; paperback ed., 2 vols., 1964; 2d ed., 2 vols., 1988

Sources of Chinese Tradition, 1960; paperback ed., 2 vols., 1964

Sources of Korean Tradition, paperback ed., vol. 1, 1997

NEO-CONFUCIAN STUDIES

Instructions for Practical Living and Other Neo-Confucian Writings by Wang Yang-ming, tr. Wing-tsit Chan 1963

Reflections on Things at Hand: The Neo-Confucian Anthology, comp. Chu Hsi and Lü Tsu-ch'ien, tr. Wing-tsit Chan 1967

Self and Society in Ming Thought, by Wm. Theodore de Bary and the Conference on Ming Thought. Also in paperback ed. 1970

The Unfolding of Neo-Confucianism, by Wm. Theodore de Bary and the Conference on Seventeenth-Century Chinese Thought. Also in paperback ed. 1975

Principle and Practicality: Essays in Neo-Confucianism and Practical Learning, eds. Wm. Theodore de Bary and Irene Bloom. Also in paperback ed. 1979

The Syncretic Religion of Lin Chao-en, by Judith A. Berling 1980

The Renewal of Buddhism in China: Chu-hung and the Late Ming Synthesis, by Chün-fang Yü 1981

Neo-Confucian Orthodoxy and the Learning of the Mind-and-Heart, by Wm. Theodore de Bary 1981

Yüan Thought: Chinese Thought and Religion Under the Mongols, eds. Hok-lam Chan and Wm. Theodore de Bary 1982

The Liberal Tradition in China, by Wm. Theodore de Bary 1983

The Development and Decline of Chinese Cosmology, by John B. Henderson 1984

The Rise of Neo-Confucianism in Korea, by Wm. Theodore de Bary and JaHyun Kim Haboush 1985

Chiao Hung and the Restructuring of Neo-Confucianism in Late Ming, by Edward T. Ch'ien 1985

Neo-Confucian Terms Explained: Pei-hsi tzu-i, by Ch'en Ch'un, ed. and trans. Wing-tsit Chan 1986

Knowledge Painfully Acquired: K'un-chih chi, by Lo Ch'in-shun, ed. and trans. Irene Bloom 1987

To Become a Sage: The Ten Diagrams on Sage Learning, by Yi T'oegye, ed. and trans. Michael C. Kalton 1988

The Message of the Mind in Neo-Confucian Thought, by Wm. Theodore de Bary 1989

Printed in the USA
CPSIA information can be obtained
at www.ICGtesting.com
JSHW021804100424
60936JS00005B/342